Psalms from Prison

Psalms from Prison

Benjamin F. Chavis, Jr.

The Pilgrim Press
Cleveland, Ohio

The Pilgrim Press, Cleveland, Ohio 44115
© 1983, 1994 by Benjamin F. Chavis, Jr.

Printed in the United States of America
The paper used in this publication is acid free

99 98 97 96 95 94   5 4 3 2 1

Library of Congress Cataloging-in-Publication Data

Chavis, Benjamin F., 1948-
Psalms from prison.
1. Meditations. 2. Prayers. 3. Prisoners—Prayerbooks
and devotions—English. I. Title.
BV4832.2.C5234 1983 242'.86 83-8026
ISBN 0-8298-0969-4 (pbk.)

In memory of Benjamin F. Chavis, Sr.,
this book is dedicated to
Elisabeth Ridley Chavis
and Charles Earl Cobb, Sr.

CONTENTS

EDITOR'S NOTE

The Reverend Benjamin F. Chavis, Jr., executive director of the NAACP and former executive director of the Commission for Racial Justice, United Church of Christ, has for over two decades been a tireless champion for racial justice in both word and deed. Wrongly imprisoned in 1972 with nine other African Americans for inciting race riots in Wilmington, North Carolina, Dr. Chavis furtively recorded his theological and ethical reflections on bits of toilet tissue and napkins in dark, cramped jail cells while awaiting his own freedom from injustice. The result, *Psalms from Prison*, is a profound testament of struggle, faith, and hope that vividly reflects Dr. Chavis's conviction that the God of the Bible is indeed a God of liberation. At once disturbing and uplifting, these words of one of America's great moral leaders are a clarion call that the fight for justice, and God's comforting presence in that fight, endures.

INTRODUCTION

A prison cell in twentieth-century America may not be an unusual place to do theology or to reflect upon one's existential understanding of Christian faith, ministry, and praxis. From the early days of the Old and New Testaments through the historical development of the Christian church, prisons have not been unusual places for those who have attempted to act out in life their belief and faith in the God of justice and liberation. Although I found the prison system in the state of North Carolina to be a viciously cruel place for a human being to be held captive, I affirm this was the place that provided me with a unique opportunity to engage in consistent struggle and reflective dialogue with God and humanity.

The history of African people in the United States of America is a history of struggle against racial oppression, injustice, and exploitation. It is a history of both the pain and the joy of the struggle for justice and liberation. The trials, tribulations, and unjust imprisonment of the Wilmington Ten in North Carolina in the 1970's challenged the church and progressive sectors of society to render a commitment to do justice. It was a historic challenge to a historic problem: racism.

As an ordained African-American minister in the United Church of Christ, I believe that the church by definition should take a stand on the side of the oppressed in the struggle for freedom. God in Christ calls the church to be involved at all levels of the liberation and progressive social-transformation process. The United Church of Christ as a denomination has the legacy of a long tradition of forthright leadership in the social-justice field. Amid the turbulence of the 1960s, the General Synod of the United Church of Christ established the United Church of Christ Commission for Racial Justice. The Commission for Racial Justice was mandated to provide leadership in mobilizing the membership of the denomination to work for racial justice. Under the leadership of Dr. Charles E. Cobb, the Commission for Racial Justice continues to be at the forefront of the struggle to end racial injustice in the United States. Together with the Ministers for Racial and Social Justice (MRSJ) and United Black Christians (UBC), the Commission for Racial Justice has had an effective impact on church and society.

The 150 psalms that I wrote while in prison in North Carolina should be viewed within the overall social context of the witness made by the United Church of Christ in general and the specific commitment of the United Church of Christ Commission for Racial Justice to combat the gross injustice imposed on the Wilmington Ten. On October 18, 1972, I and Anne Shepherd and nine Black student leaders—Marvin Patrick, Connie Tindall, Jerry Jacobs, Willie Earl Vereen, James McKoy, Reginald Epps, Wayne Moore, and Joe Wright—were sentenced to a combined total of 282 years in prison for alleged "unlawful burning" and "conspiracy to assault" in 1971 in Wilmington, North Carolina. Although we all were completely innocent of these false charges, we were convicted and sent to prison as a result of a systematic frame-up by state and federal authorities. It should be noted that the racial strife in Wilmington, North Carolina and our subsequent arrest and trial occurred during the height of President Richard Nixon's national "law and order" campaign.

In February 1971, the Commission for Racial Justice dispatched me to Wilmington, North Carolina to give organizational assistance to the pastor, members, and surrounding community of Gregory Congregational United Church of Christ. This church had become the central meeting place for Black high school students and their parents who assembled to address the continued violent, racist attacks on Black students attempting to attend desegregated local schools. At that time, I was the Coordinator for Community Organization for the NC/VA Field Office of the Commission for Racial Justice. The church soon came under violent attack from racist vigilante groups, such as the Ku Klux Klan (KKK) and the Rights of White People (ROWP). The Rev. Eugene Templeton, pastor of Gregory Congregational Church, the Rev. Leon White, director of the NC/VA Field Office of the United Church of Christ Commission for Racial Justice, and I appealed to local and state officials for "law and order" to stop the violence of the vigilantes. Our appeals, however, were to no avail. Wilmington went to the brink of full racial warfare, and the state reacted during the ensuing year by officially accusing the victims of the violence of responsibility for the Wilmington riot. This situation was similar to a riot that occurred in Wilmington in 1898. It was out of a historical context of racial conflict that the infamous case of the Wilmington Ten arose.

Our imprisonment in various county jails and state prisons in 1972 and later from 1976 to 1979 provided the setting for considerable contemplation of the vital questions of justice, human rights, and freedom. We were able to observe firsthand the institutionalization of racism and exploitation behind prison walls. The fact of our innocence of the false charges only made us more determined to fight for freedom. No one could have imagined that it would take millions of dollars and nearly a decade of struggle to win a victory in the Wilmington Ten case. But one thing was clear from the first day of confinement: We had to keep the faith in our God, our people, and our people's collective will and yearning to be free.

I became increasingly conscious of the importance of trying to document as much of the experience of prison as possible. The prison cell became a place to do theology as a critical function of the ongoing freedom movement. In other words, I wanted to strive to extract from that experience whatever lessons were possible for future theory and practice. Throughout my imprisonment, I managed to record in writing most of my theological and ethical reflections. These were expressed in several literary forms: prayers, laments, meditations, exaltations, critical interrogations, poetry, prophetic prose, doxology, and liturgy.

There were numerous attempts by prison authorities to confiscate or destroy my writings, so I wrote cryptically on toilet tissue and paper napkins, and sometimes I wrote prayers on the bottom of the plastic cover of the bed mattress that I slept on. During visiting hours or through the mail I would send the writings to my home in Oxford, North Carolina. At other times, fellow prisoners would hide the writings wherever they could find a safe place.

Prisons in the United States are institutions of state terrorism, hatred, violence, cruelty, and dehumanization. The prisons of North Carolina are like the national norm: overcrowding, excessive noise, poor or no lighting, brutality from guards, and decadent, filthy, rat-infested, ten-by-five-foot prison cells or large warehouse cell blocks.

After being paroled from prison in December 1979 I entered the Doctor of Ministry degree program at Howard University

Divinity School in Washington, DC. I decided at that time to compile and arrange my prison writings into a book of psalms to be the basis of a Doctor of Ministry project. Since that time I have reread these psalms many times. I have not been tempted to alter the original content or style.

Why a book of psalms? First, the book of Psalms in the Old Testament is one of the books of the Bible that is widely read, memorized, and recited in the religious tradition of the Black Church in America. The message of a psalm can be universal and at the same time speak to a particular sociohistorical context. Second, *Psalms from Prison* not only documents a particular experience, but also reveals the reality of the sustaining grace and liberating activity of God in Jesus Christ. These psalms speak directly to the issues of Black oppression, struggle, and liberation. These psalms also speak to the overall issue of human rights and human liberation in light of the gospel of Jesus Christ. Through these psalms, I have labored to speak the simple truth about the plight of the poor and oppressed. Questions are raised in these psalms about the interrelated evils of racism, capitalism, and imperialism.

The five different North Carolina prisons where I was held captive for nearly four years are as follows: Central Prison, Raleigh; Caledonia State Prison Farm, Tillery; McCain State Prison, McCain; Asheboro State Prison, Asheboro; and Hillsborough State Prison, Hillsborough.

EXPLANATION OF FORMAT AND STYLE

The book is divided into three parts: Oppression, Struggle, and Liberation.

Part I has 28 psalms. The word oppression was used to designate Part I because the social state of Black America is an oppressed state. The note at the top of each psalm tells where the prayer was uttered. Part I has a free-line style, in which each line is a single thought pattern.

Part II, consisting of psalms 29-115, was written inside Central Prison and McCain State Prison, July 1976-June 1978. The word struggle was used to characterize Part II because faith in the God of justice, love, and freedom involves a lifelong struggle to end injustice, hate, and oppression. Additionally, struggle is the logical and necessary response to oppression. The style in Part II is similar to that of the book of Psalms in the Old Testament, a free-verse style in which the verses are united in a single prayer utterance. Psalms 75-85 were written while I was on a protest spiritual-fast, refusing all food for 131 days inside McCain and Central prisons in 1976.

Part III, consisting of psalms 116-150, was written inside Hillsborough State Prison, July 1978-December 1979. The word liberation was used to designate Part III because, in my opinion, the essential message of the gospel of Jesus Christ is liberation. The hope of the oppressed, the faith of those who are in struggle for freedom, all find fulfillment in the sustaining and liberating grace of God in Christ. The style is similar to that of Part I.

The psalms speak for themselves. Although each psalm was written inside a prison cell, it is my prayer that the theological and ethical message of the psalms will not be imprisoned or confined to a narrow interpretation. The context is particular, but the message is universal.

Benjamin F. Chavis, Jr.
1983

PART I

Oppression

Wilmington, NC: Morning of reincarceration of
the Wilmington Ten, February 2, 1976

Blessed Are the People Oppressed

O God
blessed are the people oppressed
in struggle for human liberation
who are weak in strength
yet strong in faith
who are persecuted and mocked
stoned and crucified
nailed to the swaggering cross of racism and injustice
yet struggling onward
through thy love.

Burgaw, NC: Inside prison bus en route to Central Prison

Hear My Prayer

Hear my prayer, O God
hear my cry, O God
relieve the painful hurt of my comrades
dry the tears of our families
render us more determination
to advance thy movement, and thy reign come
as we are kidnapped away to the inhuman dungeons
by the ruthless hands of our persecutors
forgive them, O God
for they know not what they do.

PSALM 3

Raleigh, NC: Inside prison bus en route to Central Prison

My Fear Is Gone

O God, although many are rising up against me
my fear is gone *Thank you being for our*
thou, O God, art my refuge
from those who wear long black robes
in the courts of repression and injustice
from those who are in delight
in my suffering *Thank you being for our*
thou, O God, art my shield
from the prison guards who anxiously
point their guns at my body
as I ride along
the paved freeways of america
en route to a western archipelago
my fear is gone.

Raleigh, NC: Central Prison

Give Me Thy Protection

Give me thy protection, O God
in the midst of my humiliation
while I am savagely stripped naked
by the standard operating procedure
of prison inhumanity
attempting to enslave
my mind, body, and spirit
protect me from the torture
that rages from cell to cell
destroying the fruit of thy creation
protect me from the voltage
of an electrical shock treatment at my body
protect me from the horror
of a behavior modification scalpel at my brain
and protect me, O God
from the institutional evil
that lurks behind the high walls of central prison
to a melody of human screams.

Raleigh, NC: Central Prison

Have Mercy

O God, have mercy
have mercy
on the oppressed *today*
O God, have mercy
on the prisoners *today*
forgive all sins
and renew our strength
O God, have mercy
have mercy
on the prisoners
fortify our resistance to human cruelty
O God, have mercy
please
have mercy.

Raleigh, NC: Central Prison

Block the Execution Corridor

Arise, O God
block the execution corridor
to the state gas chamber
stop the poisonous death fumes
from entering the nostrils of the condemned
. . . yes, I can see from my cell
on A-block in central prison
the corridor door of capital punishment
leading to the government legalized chamber of murder
. . . yes, inside the very cell that I am now in
many have awaited their lethal fate
in passing through that door and down the hall
never to return . . .
O God, arise and forevermore
block the execution corridor.

Raleigh, NC: Central Prison

How Long Will These Walls Stand?

O God
how long will these walls stand
with the mortar of human blood and flesh
the walls of central prison
that were erected to defile thy creation and love
stone bricks elevated high into the sky
enclosing a perimeter of vengeance and suffering
administered by the unjust of society
pretending to correct and rehabilitate
yet destroying the souls of those captive
behind the tall walls
with high-voltage electricity atop
to execute all who try to escape
the misery contained within
the century-old fortress of oppression
where these walls stand
how long?

Raleigh, NC: Central Prison

Even as I Sleep Tonight

O God my God
even as I sleep tonight
inside a cold steel cell
I feel the comfort of thy warmth
through my faith in thee
I dream of freedom
and an end to the oppression of people
I dream of worldwide peace
and the establishment of a universal brotherly
        and sisterly love now on earth
as I awake at the morning dawn
liberated through thy grace and power
I will continue to keep the faith.

Raleigh, NC: Central Prison

Help Us to Survive

O God our God
help us to survive
the castigation of our souls
by an inhuman system of incarceration
that prevails across the land
help us to survive
the debilitation of our lives
by a vicious department of correction
that operates in every state
help us to survive
the wretchedness inside the atticas
the san quentins and the central prisons
O God
help us to survive
help us to struggle
to liberate
to bring justice to all
to unite humanity upright
to bring peace on earth
and to share in thy ultimate love.

Raleigh, NC: Central Prison

Prevent the Flood

Prevent the flood, O God
prevent the flood of oppression
from engulfing thy people
relieve the pressure
from the high-powered water hose
used in central prison
to strike fear and evil at our hearts
by the forceful flow which peels the skin off our backs
as we lie in our cells
maneuvering to escape the sinful flood
to thee, O God
we pray for relief.

Asheboro, NC: Asheboro Prison Unit

We Are Herded like Sheep

O God
we are herded like sheep
inside a slaughter pen
hundreds grouped en masse
like our foregenerations in the open colosseum
ready to be singled out for a particular fate
while we wait
for our names to be called out over the loudspeaker
to board another prison bus
in destination for a slave-labor camp
but thou, O God, art our strength
we shall not become weak in faith
for we shall endure and overcome
the oppressiveness of the asheboro prison barnyard
inside a slaughter pen herded like sheep
O God
deliver us
from this amphitheater of inclemency.

Asheboro, NC: Asheboro Prison Unit

What Course Should We Take?

O God our God
what course should we take
crowded into the prison bus
the old and the young
the fearless and the afraid
wondering what course to partake
to hate and submit
or to love and rebel
we need thy guidance
help us
to see the light of our mission
in pilgrimage on the road
to the concentration camp.

PSALM 13

Tillery, NC: Caledonia Prison Farm

Hearken to the Cries

O God my God
hearken to the cries
of enslaved convicts
prisoners of an unjust society
in the fields of caledonia prison plantation
under fear of shotgun pellets from mounted
      gestapo horsemen
the armed field masters enforcing the labor of
      the workers
from dawn to dusk
to the profit of dixieland slave masters
in prayer I shout
O God my God
hearken to the cries.

Tillery, NC: Caledonia Prison Farm

Thou Art My Cosigner

O God
thou art my cosigner
on the document that I am being forced to sign
stating, "my life is not in danger at caledonia prison"
surely my only safety
rests not by my signature alone
on a state memorandum
but through thy power I shall not be harmed
for thou art with me
in struggle for freedom.

PSALM 15

Lead Us to Freedom

Lead us to freedom, O God
lead us to freedom, O God
we will follow only thee to victory
for thou art our guiding light
as we march at the edge of night
in long columns around majestic guard towers
where the taskmasters are perched in the eagle's nest
ready to snipe at our humble flesh
O God
in the earthly procession of human injustice
we know that we will be freed only by thy forceful hand
O God
lead us forever on
until thy ultimate victory is won.

Tillery, NC: Caledonia Prison Farm

Thou Art Our Bridge

O God
thou art our bridge
over the troubled waters
of the roanoke river
rapids rushing through the fertile blood-red farmlands of
    caledonia
where human bodies are daily bent down in oppressive
    subjugation
O God
rescue our souls
thou art our bridge
over the deep waters of racism and exploitation
O God
thou art our salvation.

PSALM 17

Tillery, NC: Caledonia Prison Farm

I Shall Not Refrain

O God
our holy father and mother
my creator
I shall not refrain
from giving thee praise and worship
even amid threats and intimidation
to halt the speaking of thy word
by the expressed orders of a state superintendent
for by thy will
I shall not submit
to the censorship of my speech
I shall continue through thy power
to proclaim liberty to the captives
I have no fear in suffering the consequences
for I rejoice in thy gift of grace.

Tillery, NC: Caledonia Prison Farm

Not Alone Am I

O my God
not alone am I
inside this punitive isolation cell
as a result of reading from the bible
to my fellow prisoners
no, I am not alone
for I can feel thy presence
thy immanence penetrates all
inside a modern electronic steel tomb
I am sealed off in what would be seclusion
but I am on my knees
in open prayer to thee
for thy counsel
and in thanksgiving for thy company.

Tillery, NC: Caledonia Prison Farm

Break the Chains

Arise, O God
arise, O mighty God
break the chains
of oppression on thy people
come forward and overthrow the wicked
arise, O my mighty God
break the chains
that have been tightened around my waist
tear away the leg-iron shackles from my ankles
shatter the handcuffs off my wrists
arise, O God
thou art my rock
thou art our might
arise, O God
and break the chains
of oppression on thy people.

Tillery, NC; Caledonia Prison Farm

Why Am I Being Persecuted?

Dear God my God
why am I being persecuted
why are thy people oppressed
in the land of the free
why are my comrades imprisoned
why am I being tortured
chained inside the rear of a truck
in exodus from the tomb at caledonia
en route to but another yonder cell
do you hear my groans
can you feel my pains
hast thou forsaken me
O God dear God
please hear the songs that I sing to thee
of persecution and iniquity
turn my sorrow into the joy of struggle
answer me, dear God
why am I being persecuted?

PSALM 21

Tillery, NC: Inside prison truck en route to Central Prison

Relieve the Bitterness

O God our God
relieve the bitterness
against the oppressor in our hearts
even though we are unjustly wronged
by the sins of racism
let not our hearts be troubled
in response by hate and violence
for our faith is in thy redemption
thou shalt dethrone the tyrants
and restore thy creation
in love and peace.

Raleigh, NC: Central Prison

Deliver Us

O God
deliver us
from the hands of the unjust
deliver us
from the clutches of evil
deliver us
from domination by the wicked
deliver us
from the modern slavery of thy people
deliver us
from the reins of political repression
O God
by thy power
deliver us
from the sins of the world.

Raleigh, NC: Inside prison truck en route to
McCain Prison Hospital

Thou Art My Shepherd

O God my God
thou art my shepherd
you are all I need
for I am but a sheep
in thy pasture
thou do lead me in safety
along the dangerous roads on earth
you are my protector
thou restores my conscience
together we are in struggle for righteousness' sake
even though I ride
through the valley of death
I am not afraid
for I have the comfort of thy company
thou do console me
amid my enemies
thou sustains my existence with love
my spirit rejoices
surely God's blessings will remain with me
and I shall live forever with God in heaven.

PSALM 24

McCain, NC: McCain Prison Hospital

We Are Patient

O God our God
we are patient
although we are experiencing an agony of despair
we shall be patient
awaiting thy judgment
we stand at thy right hand
steadfast in our faith in thee
we shall endure the torment of dehumanization
for our perseverance is essential in these trying times
although the transgressors are building empires
we are patient
because they shall surely fall
O God our God
we are as patient as Job.

McCain, NC: McCain Prison Hospital

Let Thy Light Shine

My God my God
let thy light shine
through the iron bars of prison
let thy powerful rays sterilize the germs of injustice
let thy light shine on the courts
because there is no justice in the land
for the poor, the meek, and the downtrodden
let thy light shine on the path of love
that I and my neighbors might follow thee
let thy light shine in my heart
that I may give of myself in action to thee
let thy light shine in the eyes of the ungodly
that they will bow to thy judgment
the truth is thy light
and thou shalt brilliantly shine forever.

McCain, NC: McCain Prison Hospital

Here Come the Drugs

O God
here come the drugs
of behavior modification
to stabilize the minds of the condemned
thorazine passed out in gallons
into the bodies of the afflicted
prolixin zombie shots injected into the veins
of the "uncontrollable" enslaved
O God
I pray for thy intervention
let thy medicine come to the unrighteous
and, O God
by thy power
heal the sickness of inhumanity.

PSALM 27

McCain, NC: McCain Prison Hospital

The Nightmare of McCain

O God my God
the nightmare of mccain
lingers before me in reality
to see, to hear, and to feel
the torturing insensitivity of prison life
it hardens my soul
for I am awakened by the scream of a suffering inmate
which is only muted by the vociferous discordant barks
of bloodhounds chasing a runaway slave
dear God my God
put an end to the nightmare of mccain
that we may dream in peace
to awake and live
and be saved.

McCain, NC: McCain Prison Hospital

Show Us the Way

O God my God
O God our redeemer
show us the way
to a new life
where there is no hate and bigotry
show us the method
of ending our oppression
by nonviolence and love
show us how to struggle
O God
show us the way to thee
for by our faith in thee
we shall clearly see thy way
and follow thee into eternity.

PART II

Struggle

We Shall Praise Our God

We shall praise our God
    by our active participation
in the struggle for righteousness and freedom.

We shall glorify our Creator
    by our nonviolent marching
in the streets of america and south africa.

We shall exalt our Judge
    by our bringing justice
to the victims of persecution.

We shall believe in our Redeemer
    by our faith
in the revelation of Jesus Christ.

Hear My Call

Hear my call, O God;
    listen to the voice of my soul.
Give ear to my prayer, O God,
    and hearken to the meditation of my heart.

Help thy people, O God;
    give aid to the oppressed.
Relieve the suffering of thy people, O God,
    and minister unto the enslaved.

Teach us how to organize, O God;
    instruct us how to unify.
Educate thy people, O God,
    and open the eyes of all humanity.

Direct us in the struggle, O God;
    be a guide to thy freedom fighters.
Command thy people, O God,
    and ordain us for the liberation movement.

Free the Wilmington Ten

Free the wilmington ten, O God;
　　set at liberty all political prisoners.
O God, liberate marvin, anne, jerry, wayne, joe, connie,
　　willie, ben, reggie, and james; rescue us from
　　injustice.

Emancipate thy people, O God;
　　deliver us from the prisons and ghettos of society.
Set free the charlotte three, O God,
　　and unshackle all the victims of racist and
　　political repression.

Free the wilmington ten, O God;
　　set at liberty all political prisoners.
O God, through struggle eradicate racism,
　　and remove the yoke on thy people.

How Sweet It Is

Right on, O God, how sweet it is
  when thy people dwell and struggle together in unity.
O God, it is like the taste of gingerbread and lemonade
  after a successful human rights demonstration.

O God, happy are we
  who have sacrificed for thy peoples' sake.
We are pleased and made whole, O God,
  to be in complete solidarity with thee.

Right on, O God, how sweet it is
  when thy people dwell and struggle together in unity.
O God, we are in delight
  because thou shalt keep us together forever.

Who Shall Overcome?

Who shall overcome, O God;
    where is there justice?
What is our purpose, O God,
    and how are we to survive?

Better is the person who loves all peoples
    than the one who hates a neighbor.
For hate and racial prejudice will cause damnation
    but through righteous struggle and love in God
    we shall overcome.

Change the venue of our trial, O God;
    remove the hanging tree of judicial repression.
Bring forth thy judgment, O God,
    because only in thee can we find ultimate justice.

We are thy creatures, O God;
    thy mighty power is eternal.
Through thy love and grace, O God,
    we shall survive the sins of the world.

The Power of the People

O God, my rock my liberator,
 thou art our might and our salvation.
O God, my light my redeemer,
 thou art the real power of the people.

Let the liberation movements of all oppressed peoples
 and the meditation of my heart be desirable by thee.
Let our struggle for humanity
 and the spirit of my soul be acceptable to thy will.

O God, my rock my liberator,
 thou art our might and our salvation.
O God, my light my redeemer,
 thou art the real power of the people.

For Thy Peoples' Sake

For thy peoples' sake, O God;
  for the cause of the oppressed we lift up our souls.
O God, for those in prison;
  and for those who are poor we go unto them with
  thy aid.

For those who live in poverty, O God;
  for those who are hungry we feed them with thy
  bread of life.
O God, for the black and the white;
  for the red, the brown, and for all thy people
  we give love in thy name.

For thy creation, O God;
  for the wonders and blessings of life we give
  thanks to thee.
O Lord, for thy mercy;
  and for the gift of thy grace we give praise to thee.

For thy peoples' sake, O God;
  for thy everlasting salvation we are in constant
  struggle.
O God, for thy peoples' sake;
  and for thy glorious redemption we are ever faithful.

Woe unto the Imperialists

Woe unto the imperialists;
　　for the wrath of almighty God
　　shall come upon them.

Woe unto those who make war for oil, diamonds, and gold;
　　for by their greed
　　shall they proliferate a nuclear hell.

Woe unto the vampire monopolists;
　　for their own blood
　　shall they suck dry.

Woe unto the imperialists;
　　for the wrath of almighty God
　　shall come upon them.

Our God Loves Justice

Do not submit to the doers of iniquity;
 be not persuaded by the unjust.
For our God loves justice;
 and the persecuted shall prevail.

Put your trust in our God;
 struggle relentlessly for justice.
For the unrighteous shall not stand;
 but the righteous shall not fall.

Be patient for our God;
 be content with God's love.
For the pilgrimage is trying;
 yet the reward is everlasting.

Let not your soul be hardened;
 be not troubled.
For our God loves justice;
 and by God's will true justice shall triumph.

Give Me the Courage

Give me the courage, O God;
   provide my spirit with thy strength.
Come unto me, O God,
   and enter my heart with thy love.

Grant me the moral fiber to speak out, O God,
   that I may take a vocal stand for justice.
Let me be thy instrument, O God,
   that I may do thy will.

In the face of intimidation, O God,
   help me to be brave.
Where there is injustice, O God,
   in thy name give me the courage to challenge it.

Make me whole, O God;
   let my personhood be active and upright.
Give me the courage, O God,
   that I may involve my total existence
   in thy liberation of humanity from sin.

PSALM 39

Woe unto Those Who Go Down
into South Africa

Woe unto those who go down into south africa
    to enslave and oppress God's people
    to exploit and steal the riches of the land
    to institute racism and apartheid—
For the wrath of almighty God shall come upon them.

The Commission for Racial Justice

Commission us, O God,
for thy struggle for racial justice.
O God, help us to implement thy programs
for helping our neighbors in need.

Ordain us, O God,
to organize thy people who are oppressed.
O God, in the national and field offices of service to thee
help us to facilitate thy will.

Appoint us, O God,
to bring about social change.
O God, help us to develop correct strategies
in our efforts to end racial discrimination.

Commission us, O God,
for thy struggle for racial justice.
O God, help us to implement thy programs
for we are pleased to be an instrumentality of thy
united church.

Blessed Are the Freedom Fighters, I

Blessed are the freedom fighters
who fight for righteousness.
For our God shall be with us
and the victory shall belong to God.

Blessed are the people
who walk the picket lines for human fairness.
For God our protector shall be with us
and we shall defeat the ungodly.

Blessed are the marchers
who march in the streets for freedom.
For God is our leader
and we shall follow forever.

False Witnesses Are Rising Up Against Us

O God, false witnesses are rising up against us;
   vicious lies are being told about our purpose.
There are those, O God,
   in government offices who conspire against us.

O God, give ear to our prayer;
   hear the agony of the cry of our distress.
O God, listen to the truth of our testimony,
   and hear the praise we give to thee.

Thou art our deliverance, O God,
   from the racist unjust courts of the land.
O God, we appeal our case to thy supreme court
   where thou art the only judge.

Vindicate us, O God,
   from political persecution and judicial repression.
O God, litigate our case in thy court
   for there is no justice for us in america.

For all oppressed peoples, O God,
   let the bells of freedom ring.
And for all political prisoners
   let the doors of the prisons swing open.

"Thou Shalt Not Kill"—
Abolish Capital Punishment

Do not break the commandment of God:
"Thou shall not kill."
For there is no law and justice
where God's law is broken.

Abolish capital punishment;
put an end to legalized murder.
For one should not take what one cannot give;
can a state or government give life?

Hear ye, all you who join with pernicious lynchers;
listen to our God.
"Thou shall not kill,"
by person nor by government.

For by your inhumane "law and order"
you dare to break God's law.
For by your virulent destruction of human life
you dare to attempt to disorder God's creation.

Be not self-deceived
by your rationalizations.
For as surely as you destroy,
you surely will be destroyed.

A Bicentennial Prayer of Repentance for the United States of America

O God our God, in the midst of the jubilant national
celebration
of the two-hundred-year birthday of the united
states of america—
I fall on my knees to thee, O God,
in a bicentennial prayer of repentance.

Although, O God, as a nation we are a superpower in
the military force
we are wealthy in capital and we are strong and
mighty—
But as a people we are immoral and greedy
we are poor in wisdom and we are weak and powerless.

Is it not time, O God,
for reflection, prayer, repentance, and corrective
action?
O God, hear my prayer to thee
for thy forgiveness of the sins of this country.

O God, forgive this country
for the genocide of native american people
for the rape and slavery of african people
and for the exploitation of poor people.

O God, forgive this country
  for violence and war
  for vietnam
  and for chile.

O God, forgive this country
  for the gas chambers
  for the firing squads
  and for the electric chairs.

O God, forgive this country
  for polluting the air
  for polluting the seas
  and for the abuse of nature.

O God, forgive this country
  for the watergates
  for the political assassinations
  and for the c i a.

O God, forgive this country
  for its trespasses
  and help the united states to forgive
  all who have trespassed against us.

Forgive this country, O God,
  and let the united states become a superpower of love
  toward all peoples
  and nations.

Whatever Happened to the Scottsboro Boys?

Whatever happened, O God,
  to the scottsboro boys?
Once there were nine black men
  down in alabama on trial for their lives.

Why were these, O God,
  innocent men crucified by the courts?
In a racist society
  was being black their crime?

What were you saying to us, O God;
  what is the meaning and lesson of that true story?
O God, do we need other vivid examples, stories, or
  parables;
  are we still asleep?

Wake us up, O God;
  arouse our spirits.
O God, forever disturb our souls
  that we may always remember what happened to the
  scottsboro boys.

Dare to Struggle

Dare to struggle, all of you who are oppressed;
  dare to take a stand for human liberty.
Confront the unrighteous;
  halt the oppression.

Be not afraid to speak out for justice;
  do not remain silent to inhumanity.
Learn to organize your people;
  teach the right way of liberation.

Employ the methods of nonviolent civil disobedience;
  proceed through the virtue of love.
March on for human rights;
  trample upon the vice of racial hatred.

Dare to struggle, all you who are oppressed;
  dare to see the everlasting light of freedom.
For almighty God, our creator,
  has made the way clear.

To Keep Martin's Dream Alive

O God, to keep martin's dream alive
  help us to become active ministers of social change.
In order to be good leaders
  help us to become good followers of thy word.

Give us the understanding;
  grant us the wisdom;
That we shall make the crooked straightforward
  and cause the blind to see thy light.

Help us to heal the sick, O God,
  and to feed the hungry;
That we shall struggle against poverty,
  and shall establish a new covenant with thee.

Let our hearts be compassionate,
  our determination solid.
By our nonviolent civil rights activity
  let us forever keep martin's dream alive.

Now Is the Time

Now is the time for freedom's quest
   the hour of liberation.
From the prison cells and county jails
   from the slums and ghettos.

The moment of struggle has arrived
   the social revolution breaks forth,
The shackles torn loose
   the chains broken.

O God, hear our plea
   give us thine aid.
To our comrades in staccato screams we shout,
   "Now is the time . . .
         now is the time . . .
            now is the time."

We Are Lost in the Wilderness

We are lost in the wilderness, O God;
  we thirst and hunger for thee.
Our lips are parched with silence;
  our souls dried up.

In the desert of hopelessness we tread
  through the hot sands of human degradation.
Wandering on the still lethargic prairies of apathy,
  thy people are lost.

Through the sins of our existence
  we have become alienated from thee.
Yet it has been through our earthly oppression
  that we have found thee in closeness.

Deliver thy people, O God;
  save us from destruction.
For it is by our faith that we shall be rescued;
  and we shall freely drink from thine oasis of love.

Defend Me

Defend me, O God
  from the awesome wanton power of the state.
O God, protect me
  from the malicious district attorney.

Be with my codefendants, O God;
  give them thy comfort.
Speed the day of our vindication;
  bring forth thy judgment.

Defend the wilmington ten, O God;
  free all political prisoners.
Protect us, O God
  from the racism of american society.

Answer my prayer, O God;
  defend me as I continue to struggle.
Let there be freedom for all peoples;
  let there be justice for all.

A Psalm of Reflection

O God, as I pray to thee
 from a cell in a north carolina prison—
Help me to reflect on my past experiences
 that I may effectively deal with the present
 in order to look clearly into the future.

For in my short life, O God,
 it has been a long struggle.
But you have been with me
 all the way through.

As I remember, O God, at six years old
 in the "colored orphanage" elementary school
 I was awakened; my conscience questioned why—
All God's children did not have shoes to wear;
 all did not have books to read.

I was enrolled in the colored school system,
 drank from the colored water fountains.
I attended the colored episcopal church,
 used the colored library.

Somewhere I was told that I was a negro,
 that I was an inferior human being.
I was ashamed of my existence,
 despised by my fellow countrymen.

Yes, O God, I really was scared
   to go into that new town library.
But I had an irresistible itch
   not to check out a book
   but to register in a protest.

Thank you, God,
   for giving me that courage.
Somehow I then began to understand and feel good
   about being a child of God,
   a black manchild of african ancestry.

I was proud of my blackness,
   grateful for my humanity.
I became determined to try to do what was right,
   to follow thy word.

Lord, don't get me wrong;
   I am not claiming to have been a saint.
Although I still remember being an altar boy in church
   every sunday for sixteen years.

I participated in the civil rights movement:
   the demonstrations, the picket lines, and the sit-ins.
I was spit on and pushed to the ground,
   cursed out and teargassed.

I prayed constantly,
   always kept the faith.
I joined c o r e, n a a c p, and s c l c,
   organized students and workers.

I became a staff person
   of the united church of Christ commission for racial
      justice.
I accepted thy call
   into thy ministry.

O my God, thou hast carried me through
   some very rough times.
Do you remember when you were with us
   as we marched in asheville, greensboro, charlotte,
   washington dc, oxford, warrenton, raleigh,
   winston-salem, and in other cities?

O God, do you remember in henderson when the police used
      the "pepper-fog machine"
   to teargas us while we were on our knees
   in prayer to thee inside davis chapel?
Do you remember in portsmouth when the police turned the
      dogs loose on us
   because we had sung "we shall overcome" at norcom
      school?
And God, I know you remember in wilmington
   when they shot up gregory congregational church.
The white supremacist vigilantes attacked us out of racist
      hate;
   the ku klux klan and the rights of white people's
      organization drew the blood of the black community.

Thank you, God,
   for helping us to survive.
For thou hast sustained us with thy love;
   thou art our hope;
   thou art our faith.

O God, even today as many of thy people are unjustly
      imprisoned
   the sin of racism continues to permeate all our society.
Governmental and economic monopolies are exploitative and
      oppressive;
   legislatures and courts have become repressive;
   and yes, even some of the religious institutions
   have become insensitive to the real needs of the poor and
      oppressed.

But thou, O God, hast shown me thy way,
   the correct method of struggle.
Thou hast reinforced my spirit,
   strengthened my soul.

Into the future I can see;
   amid the cosmic storm I can hear.
From thee, O God, the vision is clear;
   thy word is perfect.

Woe unto the unrighteous,
   for you shall fall into the abyss of hell.
Behold, you people oppressed,
   the faithful and the righteous,
   for in the end you shall be saved.

I Believe in Miracles

Listen to my testimony, O God;
   hear the truth of my heart.
I believe in miracles,
   for I have witnessed thy miraculous power.

Thou art my ultimate source,
   my undergirding force.
Through thy power, O God,
   I have walked through the fire of human hate unharmed.

In the midst of our persecution
   I am confident that thou wilt deliver us.
My physical body may be in chains
   but thou hast freed my spirit.

The spirit of thy people has always been stronger
   than the will of the oppressor.
For our present suffering will in the end be our salvation;
   our struggle shall bring our liberation.

To some, O God, it seems a hopeless situation,
   an unattainable goal.
But we have faith in thee, O God;
   we shall be freed by thy power.

In Memory of Steve Mitchell

O God, my creator,
    I offer this prayer—
In memory of steve mitchell
    who in 1971 at the age of seventeen
    was slain by a wilmington policeman's bullet.

A black high school student leader, O God,
    who was loving toward all.
A young freedom marcher
    who was helping the community.

When he came out of a church to pull a fire alarm
    instantly he was fatally wounded
    and dragged by his heels to a squad car.
Somehow the law investigated,
    called it justifiable homicide.

I pray, O God,
    for thy inquest.
Let the truth be told
    about the murder of our brother.

O God, on the outskirts of town
    in an overgrown grassy cemetery field
    another one of thy sons lies.
Peace be unto his soul,
    eternal freedom his spirit.

In remembrance of him
    let us rededicate ourselves to struggle for freedom.
May his death be not in vain,
    his life not forgotten.

Blessed Are Thy People Who Cry

Blessed are thy people who cry,
   who moan and groan for relief
   in struggle for liberation.
For God our ultimate liberator
   shall bring to pass an end to oppression;
   our tears of sorrow shall become tears of joy.

Blessed are those who suffer,
   who are in pain and torture
   because of inhumanity.
For God our holy comforter
   shall terminate the agony;
   our wounds shall be healed.

Blessed are thy people who mourn,
   who lament and weep over
   the cruel state of our existence.
For God our sustaining redeemer
   shall deliver those who cry out for God's help;
   through God our fate is assured.

Blessed are those who are patient,
   who struggle on relentlessly
   having complete faith in God.
For God our liberator and salvation
   shall always be on time.

Sing Songs of Cheer

Behold, all you in struggle for freedom,
in struggle against injustice.
Sing songs of cheer;
shout chants of exultation to God.

As we march in the streets of soweto and johannesburg,
stepping up the pace we proceed through the southland of
america.
Hear our songs, O God;
O God, give ear to our jubilation as we continue
to fight in thy name.

The harmony of our voices in solidarity,
the attunement and unison of the movement's spirituals
have a message:
We rejoice for we only fear God;
therefore we shall not be moved and we shall not be
silent.

Our music is universal;
common songs of the oppressed we sing.
All glory be to God;
praise God by active participation in humanity's quest for
freedom.

PSALM 56

I Give Thanks to Thee

O gracious God, I give thanks to thee;
    my soul is in humble gratitude for thy uplifting spirit.
For all the blessings of my life,
    for the good feeling of thy consoling power
    my soul rejoices.

For thy revealing light, O God,
    and for the lessons of my experiences I am grateful.
Thou hast enabled me to endure the torturing confinement of
      prison;
    my convictions of struggle have not weakened
    for my faith in thee has only become stronger.

It is with a satisfying emotion, O God,
    that I fall routinely on my knees in prayer to thee.
I am in constant dialogue with thee;
    thou hast spoken to the depths of my consciousness
    and my heart attempts to reciprocate thy love.

Come into Wilmington, NC

Hear us, O God;
    hearken to our desperate plea.
Come into wilmington, nc;
    let thy light shine on this repressive port city.

Thy people here are in need, O God;
    we call out for thy aid.
Get us together;
    encourage thy people to organize for liberation.

On the waterfront of the cape fear
    help us to stand up for that which is right in thy sight.
Years ago we came to these same indelicate wooden docks
    on slave ships chained as property en route to the
        open-air market.

And today, O God, the shackles of poverty and injustice
    are welded on thy people with the phlegmatic steel of
        indifference.
Some of us have given up;
    there is no hope left in their being.
But thou, O God, art the greatest of hopes;
    thou art our strength.
Come unto us and grant thy people an awakening;
    come into wilmington and let thy light shine
    on all thy creation.

Let Thy Workers of the World Unite

I pray, O God, for the unity of all working people
　　in struggle to prevent the exploitation of their labor.
Let thy workers of the world unite;
　　let all thy people share in the fruits of humanhood.

Thou art our shop steward, O God;
　　thou art our representative before all unscrupulous
　　　　corporate managements.
Let us work for thy salvation;
　　let us put a stop to human slavery.

O God, help us to tear down the barrier of racism
　　which is used to divide thy people.
Let the multitudes of workers both black and white
　　see the necessity to join hands together in struggle.

Bring us to unity, O God;
　　for we are all sisters and brothers.
Let our collective energies restore peace among all nations;
　　let thy workers of the world unite!

Greater Is the Spirit of the Oppressed

Greater is the spirit of the oppressed
   than the wickedness of tyrannical slave drivers.
For those who oppress shall bite the dust of defeat;
   but God shall bring liberation to the downtrodden.

Stronger are the pure in heart
   than those who exist in human hate.
For the subjugative desires of the oppressors shall not
      prevail;
   yet God shall make the burdened strong.

Better is God's blessing to the poor in need
   than the self-destructive curse of the rich in greed.
For rather than the rapacious despots of wall street
   it is God who determines the created destiny of the
      people.

In Prayer for Eugene and Donna Templeton

Hear me, O God,
>for I beseech thee to hear the voice of my soul.

I come, O Lord,
>in prayer for eugene and donna templeton.

Bless them, O God,
>for their courage and righteousness.

Protect them from all evil;
>shield them from all harm.

In wilmington when others were afraid, O God,
>they stood up for thee.

And through the many tribulations
>their faith in thee remains strong.

O God, be with them now and forever;
>for eugene and donna continue to work in thy name.

Let thy sustaining love console them;
>and may they receive thy gift of grace.

Thy Church Became Under Siege

O God, inside the gregory congregational church
    we were a community fellowship in worship to thee,
    singing spirituals and freedom songs.
It was a very difficult time, O God,
    for we were struggling to promote an equal quality
        education for black youth;
    however to prevent that—thy church became under siege.

We were surrounded by race-prejudiced vigilantes,
    attacked by bloodthirsty civilians
    and wounded from sniper shots.
We pleaded with local officials for police protection,
    begged for a curfew
    but all to no avail.

Yet it was in these circumstances, O God,
    that you came to our rescue,
    enabled us to survive.
When reverend templeton faithfully called on thee,
    as patricia rhodes eloquently screamed for thee
    and while I humbly prayed to thee—
Thou didst come;
    and when thy church became under siege
    thou, O God, didst save us all.

I Put My Trust in Thee

O God my God, my soul longs for thee;
   my heart beats to thy will.
I put my trust in thee, O God;
   I yearn to celebrate thy love.

O God, thou art my confidence;
   thou art my only ray of hope.
Before the dangers of society
   thou art my security.

O God, I do accept thy call;
   I shall preach thy word.
In constant struggle for thy kingdom
   I put my trust in thee.

In My Distress

In my distress, O God,
    from a dark prison cell in america
    I urgently summon thy aid.
O God, I am in misery;
    inside a filthy feculent north carolina dungeon
    my spirit awaits thy disburdening relief.

For thou hast assured me, O God;
    thou hast made me confident
    that thy deliverance is near.
Grant me the determination,
    render me the stamina
    to make it through this ungodly journey on earth.

An African Congregation

O God our God, in thy name we established
   an african congregation,
   a vanguard church in struggle.
Our efforts were in response
   to the black christian nationalist movement;
   for we were young, black, and proud to be thy creatures.

But then, O God, it seemed to us
   that most formal religions had been used
   only as a tool of oppression.
Therefore we attempted to redefine,
   to rediscover our existence in terms of our ancestry
   and in terms of the living reality of thy love and ultimacy.

Yet, O God, it was through that experience,
   through our spiritual development
   and the many hard lessons learned—
We all came to appreciate,
   to love and struggle for all thy people
   regardless of race, creed, and color.

Kojo Nantambu

O God, give my brother thy protection;
　provide him with thy wisdom.
Kojo nantambu, O God,
　　"unconquerable black man of destiny"
　　in struggle for freedom's sake.

O God, let thy spirit
　　pour into his heart;
　　let thy power fortify his soul.
A native of wilmington struggling
　　through the modern jungles of oppression.

Watch over kojo, O God;
　　lead him safely along the dangerous streets
　　and may thy will be done.
O God, help him to follow thee
　　that he may help thy people.

Give Me Thy Mercy

Give me thy mercy, O God;
    restore my soul.
Come into my heart;
    enter my bloodstream
    and replenish my body.

O merciful God, I love thee;
    I exist by thy will
    and live for thy salvation.
Let me forever work for thee
    until thy great victory is won.

Forgive me, O God,
    for all my wrongdoings,
    for not following thy word.
Give me thy mercy;
    let my life be always for thy purpose.

Molly and Leatrice Hicks

O God, hear this psalm;
   give ear to my testimony
   and listen to our prayers for justice.
Molly and leatrice hicks,
   a black mother and daughter in struggle for freedom,
   were persecuted because of their leadership and
      involvement in the civil rights movement.
O God, molly, leatrice, and I
   were the wilmington three;
   together we suffered the torment of a racist prosecutor.
We were falsely accused, indicted, and arrested;
   ridiculed, slandered, and jailed.
The intense wickedness and hatred around us
   caused a tremendous pressure on our souls.
And, O God, because of the inhuman pressure
   my dear sister molly suffered a nervous breakdown;
   I must confess that the situation became almost insufferable.

Yet, my God, you were there when we needed you most;
   you came to our deliverance
   and you revived our souls with thy spirit.
Although the trauma of that experience still lingers today,
   we understand this history in the illumination
   of the historic suffering and struggle of our people.
May thine eternal blessings always be upon molly and
      leatrice and may we all find renewed faith in thee.
May we all remember the strength of Molly
   even unto the final hour.

Woe unto the Unjust Courts

Woe unto the unjust courts
   where the poor are victimized
   where people of color are lynched
   where political activists are sentenced to prison.
For the wrath of almighty God shall come upon them.

Woe unto the judges
   who render racist judgments
   who try to play god
   who are cruel and inhumane.
For the wrath of almighty God shall come upon them.

Woe unto the juries
   that find innocent people guilty
   that vote to take human life
   that partake in political repression
For the wrath of almighty God shall come upon them.

I Yearn for Thy Love

O God, my God and savior,
    thou art the breath of my soul,
    the essence of my spirit.
I yearn for thy love;
    I long for thy salvation.

O God, my God and creator,
    thou art the foundation of my existence,
    the undergirding force of my life.
I yearn for thy love;
    I long for thy liberation.

We Are the Wilmington Ten

O God, we are innocent victims
of a racist and political prosecution.
O God, we are the wilmington ten;
hear our prayer
and let not our persecution continue.

Come into our prison cells, O God;
break loose the chains and shackles.
O God, we are the wilmington ten;
listen to our plea
for in america we are political prisoners of conscience.

Because we dared, O God,
to speak out for thy people
and to say no to racial discrimination—
We were arrested in wilmington,
jailed and teargassed in the new hanover county jail.

O God, we are the wilmington ten;
please give ear to our cry:
"free all u.s. political prisoners."
Let thy wrath and power come
upon the virulent racist courts of north carolina.

O God, marvin patrick, connie tindall, jerry jacobs,
   anne shepherd, willie vereen, james mckoy,
   reginald epps, wayne moore, joe wright, and I
   are the wilmington ten.
We have been sentenced to a total
   of 282 years in prison.

But our faith in thee, O God, causes us
   even from behind the prison walls not to give up;
   we fight on for righteousness.
The imprisonment of freedom fighters
   shall not stop the freedom movement of thy people.

For time is on our side
   and by thy will through mass struggle
   we all shall be set free.
O God, we are the wilmington ten;
   we give thanks for thy love
   and we pledge to continue to wage thy liberation
   struggle.

Assist Our Defense Lawyers

O God, assist our defense lawyers;
  lend thy help to our legal counsel
  before the bar of southern injustice.
For here the courtrooms are no longer
  halls of equal justice under the law.

Give thy aid, O God;
  render thy hand in favor of the oppressed.
Argue along with our attorneys
  against the iniquities before us;
  join in our plea to the court.

"Your honor, we object," we constantly shout;
  "we object to racism,
  we object to human exploitation,
  we object to judicial repression,
  and we object to all violations of human rights."

O God, we pray for justice;
  we scream for truth.
Come into this courtroom, O God,
  and assist our defense lawyers;
  give aid to attorney ferguson and our other lawyers.

A Prayer for Allen Hall

O God, I am back on my knees
   in humble prayer to thee.
Hear me, O God;
     listen to this psalm I pray
     for a brother who has been misused and abused.

A prayer for allen hall, O God,
     I give in all honesty.
Although my brother was used by the state
     to get on a witness stand to give false testimony against us
     I have no hate in my heart toward him.

O God, I pray that you will comfort his soul,
     bring warmth to his spirit,
     and restore his life in goodness.
For he has repented for his sin;
     he has recanted his false testimony.

Free all victims, O God,
     of inhuman trickery and abuse.
Free allen hall from the clutches of the sheriff's deputies;
     free him from his prison cell
     and let thy love surround and protect him.

Prison Would Be Hell

Without thee, O God,
    without thy love
    prison would be hell.
The misery of prison puts a wrenching test on my faith;
    my heart is hardened;
    my spirit is petrified.

Sometimes I feel lost in the shadows of hate,
    angry about the horrid captivity of my body
    and afraid of the uncertainty of life.
But from the flush four corners of my prison cell
    thy love radiates and converges at the innermost vertex of
        my soul;
    my suffering abates.

The scorching fires of inhumanity rage;
    the smoldering coals of persecution flame up
    at the torrent winds of racism.
Yet, O God, it is here that I am sustained by thee
    and consoled by thy spirit;
    because without thy love
    prison would be hell.

I Am Compelled to Protest

O God, my God and might,
　　thou art the light of the world
　　and the only muscle of my strength.
There is evil all around me;
　　in the face of twentieth-century slavery
　　I am compelled to protest.

Let not my voice, O God,
　　become silent to racial injustice.
Let me react not by violence
　　but let me act morally
　　and forthrightly in a peaceful manner
　　to protest the sinful conditions of the world.

Speak to me, O God;
　　tell me what to do.
Struggle with me, O God;
　　for I must take a stand—
　　I can no longer silently tolerate
　　the yoke on my soul.

Fast for Justice and Human Rights

Today, O God, I do come in solemn prayer
    for I now begin to fast for justice and human rights.
Let thy spirit overtake my soul
    as I give up all food
    in a serious moral effort
    to awaken thy people.

I shall not eat the roach-infested food
    offered by the hands of the unjust.
I shall not drink the blood
    of the vampires of monopoly interests.
I shall not obey the demands
    of ruthless prison authorities.

O God, there is no fear in my heart
    as I enter the twilight of righteousness
    through thy spirit.
I only hunger for thee, O God;
    I only thirst for thy love;
    and I only desire justice and freedom
    for all thy people.

"Is Not This Fast. . . ?"

O God, is not this fast
    that I struggle
    to break the chains of oppression,
    to tear down the walls of racism,
    to bring liberty to the enslaved,
    and to free political prisoners?

Doing my fast for justice, O God,
    I am made whole in spirit;
    I am made more concerned for those who are hungry;
    for those who do not have food to give up;
    for the impoverished
    and for the malnourished.

O Lord, let me not yield to temptation,
    but strengthen my determination.
Remove the sour tastes from my mouth;
    relieve my swollen tonsils
    and ease the cramps in my stomach.

Let this fast, O God,
    be for thy purpose.
Is not this fast for human liberation?

For Twenty-one Days

O God, my God and creator,
   rejuvenate my body;
   rekindle my spirit.
For twenty-one days
   I continue to fast
   for thy salvation and freedom.

The hunger pains and stomachaches
   have now completely disappeared;
   my mouth is no longer dry.
O God, I feel like I have never felt before;
   I sense the oneness of thy creation
   and the ultimacy of thy power.

Help me, O God, to continue
   to increase my awareness of these
   as I continue to fast.
Thank you, O God, for allowing me
   to approach thee
   and understand the reality of thy being.

For Forty-nine Days

O God, my God my strength,
  thou art the source of my life,
   the conscience of my soul.
For forty-nine days
   I continue to fast
   for thy liberation.

I am in a prison bed
   inside central prison hospital
   where I have laid my burdens upon thy shoulders.
My faith in thee grows stronger;
   my love for thee leaps out from my heart;
   my soul is at rest.

O God, bless my family
   for they worry about my health;
   they are afraid of my death.
Give my loved ones hope, O God;
   let them know I am safely in thy hands;
   for I shall not now die
   but by thy will
   live to fast even longer.

In Reverent Meditation

In reverent meditation, O God,
    in devout contemplation of thee
    I offer a prayer for justice.
Lead me on, dear God,
    beside the perilous waters of american racism.

O God, I beseech thee
    to hear the cry of my heart,
    to listen to the call of my soul.
The subconscious of my spirit
    supplicates in humbleness for thy salvation.

On the spiritual plane, O God,
    I reach out for thy helping hand;
    I ponder and meditate for thy relief.
O God, I have faith in thee;
    my trust is only in thy power.

On Bended Knee

On bended knee, O God,
    I constantly pray to thee
    for an end to human exploitation and tyranny
    on earth.
I believe in prayer, O God;
    I know that you do hear
    and shall answer the cries of thy people oppressed.

O God, deliver us
    from the prison dungeons;
    free us from institutional slavery.
Deliver us, O God,
    from the urban cement ghettos
    and from the "new south" plantations.

On bended knee, O God,
    I constantly pray to thee
    for thy love and peace.

For Seventy-seven Days

O God, my hope my sustainer,
    I lift up my soul to thee;
    my body lives by thy grace.
For seventy-seven days
    by thy spirit and power
    I continue to fast.

I have come to understand, O God,
    that it is not the mere length of a fast that is important,
        but it is the confessional honesty and sincerity of one's
        heart that unites one with thine ultimate purpose.
O God, through my fast I have developed a seventh sense,
    a transcending perception of thy being.

My perception of thee,
    O God,
        is love.

For One Hundred Days

O God, my God,
  thou art the giver of life,
  the beginning and ending of time.
For one hundred days
  I continue to fast
  for justice and human rights.
O God, you have brought me through the storm;
  you have saved my soul;
  and you have blessed my life.
Is it the water or orange juice I drink
  that keeps me alive?
Or is it my faith
  in thy miraculous power?

O God, my God,
  let my life be for righteousness;
  and let my spirit abide by thy will.

Through Ascetic Practice

O God, through ascetic practice
I come to thee
in prayer and sacrifice for thy freedom.
O God, thou art my fortress,
the strength of the oppressed,
the eternal peace of life.

Help me, O God,
to endure to the end of time,
to the beginning of truth.
In self-denial, O God,
I come to thee
in prayer and sacrifice for thy peoples' sake.

O God, take complete possession of my soul;
extract from my existence all selfishness and egotism;
empty my body
that I may be filled
with thy loving spirit.

Carry Me Back

O God, at the vanguard
  I long to actively participate
  in thy freedom movement.
Carry me back, O God,
    to the dirt roads of granville county,
    to the narrow trails of zimbabwe;
    let me join the liberation front
    of thy freedom fighters.

Let me return to the exploitative factories
    to organize thy workers,
    back to the fields of caledonia
    to free the prisoner slaves.
Carry me back, O God,
    to chile and to palestine;
    to puerto rico and to namibia;
    let me join thy worldwide struggle
    for justice and human rights.

For One Hundred Thirty Days

O God, my God and holy comforter,
thou art the light of my soul,
the essence of my life.

For one hundred thirty days
through my faith in thee
I continue to fast.

There are many clear visions, O God,
that you enable me now to see:
—the suffering oppressed throughout the world shall soon
be liberated
—thy love shall conquer human hate
—peace shall be restored on earth
O God, I can see that all is possible through the collective
mass struggle of thy people in faith and action in thy
name.

At the conclusion of this fast and prayer, O God,
let me arise to act steadfastly for thy peoples' sake;
let my soul be ever active for thy salvation of all
humanity.

Thy United Front at Cairo

To thee, O God, I do call;
   hear my prayer;
   listen to the voice of my soul.
I pray for thy wisdom;
   grant an understanding of thy word
   among thy people in struggle for freedom.

Where the mighty mississippi and ohio rivers
   rush to collide in southern illinois,
   down in the valley at pyramid courts—
Where thy people are gathered in action
   let the world learn from the liberating solidarity
   of thy united front at cairo.

Sisters and brothers joined together
   in unity for righteousness,
   standing up against oppression—
Rev. charles koen following thy light,
   leading thy people through bullets, hardship, and
      despair;
   I pray, O God, for their continued survival.

Whom Shall I Fear?

God almighty is my protector,
  my guide and my liberator.
Whom shall I fear?
  to whom shall I submit?

Though the vast powers of a state
  encamp against my soul,
  I am not afraid.
Amid the quicksands of injustice
  I shall not sink.

I have put my faith in thee, O God;
  my life is in thy hand.
Protect me from sophisticated lynchers;
  guide me through inhuman treachery;
  liberate me from prison.

I cry out to thee, O God;
  I shout for freedom.
Thou art my God;
  to thee I give all praise.

Struggle with the Tuscarora

O God, my God our God,
    hear our plea;
    lend thine ear to our cause.
Struggle with the tuscarora;
    liberate all indian peoples;
    bring freedom to thy native americans.

Let our government and people repent
    for the past and present sins
    of calculated and deliberate physical, cultural, and
        spiritual genocide committed against the tuscarora and
        millions of other indian peoples of this land.

In the pursuit of civilization (?)
    we have become uncivilized,
    alienated through sin from thee—
    we attempt to write a national history
    to hide and cover up these sins.
Yet, O God, nothing can be hidden from thee;
    we pray for thy salvation;
    struggle with the tuscarora.

Blessed Are the Faithful

Blessed are the faithful,
   those who have complete allegiance to God
   in unfailing devotion.
For the faithful shall endure forever;
   in spirit they shall not perish
   but shall live eternally.

Blessed are those who confess their sins,
   who in repentance pray to God
   for the remission of unrighteousness.
For those who ask for God's forgiveness
   shall be forgiven
   and shall be saved.

Blessed are those who trust in God,
   who are true believers
   in God's ultimate being.
For the veracity and steadfastness of one's heart,
   the moral courage abiding in one's soul,
   and the total reliance of one's spirit on God's power and
      love brings and assures the blessings of the God of all.

But Help Me to Study

O God my God, let me not waste my time
   on the vanities of life:
   the lusts and frailties of societal endeavors.
But help me to study,
    to search and to understand thy word
    that I may minister unto thy people.

Help me, O God,
    to submerge my conscience into thy scriptures,
    into the testaments and good news of thy love.
In the seminaries and schools of religion
    and even in my prison cell
    let me be in dialogue with thee, O God—
Through prayer and study, O God,
    let me learn how to correctly follow thee
    in action for the liberation of thy people.

Free the Charlotte Three

Free the charlotte three, O God;
    set free our brothers:
    jim grant, t.j. reddy, and charlie parker.
O God, by thy power prevent the continued victimization
    of these our brothers
    under the vicious repression of unjust courts.

O God, protect our human rights;
    shield us from racial oppression
    and may we all find our liberation in thee.
Let the charlottee three be free, O God,
    free all political prisoners
    and break the yoke of discrimination and injustice
    on thy people.

Grant, we beseech thee, O God,
    that our struggle for human justice
    shall not be in vain.
May thy blessings be always upon
    the movement of thy people
    in struggle for freedom.

To End World Hunger

Hear our call, O God,
> listen to our prayer.

O God, we come to thee in distress;
> we humble ourselves before thee
> as we pray for thy relief and salvation.

For on earth today, O God,
> millions of thy people are hungry;
> multitudes of thy people are starving.

O God, let us unify and struggle
> to end world hunger.

For we are thankful to thee, O God,
> for the beauty and bounty of thy creation;
> for thou hast provided plenty of food for now and
> for all generations to come.

But it is because of the sins of imperialism and centuries of
> exploitative greed that a desperate few have monopolized
> the world's resources away from the masses of thy people,
> which has caused a great world to suffer and hunger.

We have faith, O God,
> that thou wilt answer our prayers,
> that thou wilt save all thy people.

We have faith, O God,
> that the righteous shall prevail,
> and that all thy people shall share equally
> in all of thy creation
> as we struggle together to end world hunger.

Our Sisters at Women's Prison

O God, our sisters at women's prison
    are in thy need;
    hear their cry for it is our cry.
Hear their prayers, O God,
    for their prayers are our prayers
    of suffering and human persecution.

For in many cases, O God,
    our sisters at women's prison
    have to go through an even more degrading experience.
We call on thee, O God,
    prevent the forced vaginal searches;
    stand in the way of the torture of our sisters.

We pray to thee, O God,
    in behalf of our sisters,
    we pray for the liberation of our mothers and daughters.
Come into women's prison, O God;
    open the cell doors
    so that our sisters and future generations can be free.

Stop the Neutron Bomb

Dear God, thou art ultimate reality;
   thou art our creator
   and the source of all living beings.
O God, thou art our hope in the face of destruction;
   thou art our comfort
   amid the threat of nuclear radiation from antihuman
      bombs.

It seems, O God,
   that the capitalists continue to value profits and property
      over human life:
   to wit the development of the death-ray bomb.
O God, through the sins of material greed
   many of our governmental leaders have become perverted
   with jubilant desires to make war by killing people and
      saving buildings.

We pray, O God,
   that by thy will the majority of thy people
   throughout the world will rise up to protest
   against this evil.

O God, help us to organize;
   help us to struggle against human extermination
   and all forms of neo-nazism.
Hear our prayer, O God:
   stop this satanic weapon;
   stop the neutron bomb.

The Handwriting upon the Wall

Behold, you rulers of the empire in the west
for God almighty has sent you a message:
for handwriting upon the wall.
For as sure as you continue to disobey God's word and law
by oppressing and exploiting the masses of God's peoples
you shall surely fall.

The eagles of modern babylon must not prey upon the
peoples of the world for in due time the wrath of God
shall encamp around them.
To the rulers of the empire in the west:
"Your days are numbered
for you have been weighed in God's balance."

Surely you are aware
that your deeds of sin have outweighed your acts of
goodness and you have put your faith in capital
as a god before God.
Surely you are aware
that you will face God's judgment
and that time is near!

Behold, the handwriting upon the wall:
"Mene, mene
tekel, upharsin."
As belshazzar fell
so will
the imperial eagle fall.

To Save Marie Hill

Dear God of our liberation, God of our creation and freedom
we struggled, prayed, and battled
to save marie hill.
We had to fight, dear God,
to save our sister
from death in the state gas chamber.

Thank you, O God, for steering
thy united church of Christ commission for racial justice
to lead that struggle in thy name.
For in north carolina
the unrighteous were determined to play god
to viciously take marie's sixteen-year life.

But through the efforts of thy ministers:
cobb, thomas, white, land, joyner, edmonds, and
others—
marie's precious life was saved.
May thy united church continue to struggle for racial justice
lest we forget
thy people oppressed.

Bless us, O God,
bless us with thy love
grant us to struggle by thy word.
Thank you, dear God,
for through thy grace
our sister lives for thee.

Lolita, Assata, and Joan

O God, God of love, God of truth and justice,
   I pray to thee for our sisters:
   lolita lebron, assata shakur, and joan little.
For these our sisters are being persecuted, imprisoned,
   and subjected to the evil reality of racism;
   but because they are strong women in struggle
   they have become even stronger in spirit.

Through the bars of their prison cells,
   let thy love comfort and sustain them
   as we on the outside see clearly the necessity
   to accelerate our collective efforts toward their freedom.
For these our sisters are symbolic of the repression of
      women who dare to take a stand against the system of
      american injustice;
   yet their strength and determination serves as an
      inspiration.

Together with these our sisters and the millions of thy
      people who are oppressed, who long and cry out for
      liberation,
   let us struggle onward.
Let us, O God, through thy love,
   through thy power
   come into a new unity:
   a new being where peace, freedom, and justice
   shall be won.

We Are Marching

Hear the sound of our feet, O God;
    listen to the tone of thy movement—
    we are marching.
Lend thine ear to our cause, dear God;
    listen to the resonance of thy people—
    we are marching.

On the highways of america,
    in the streets of south africa
    we are marching.
We are marching for human rights;
    for our God is the one true God of righteousness and
        goodness,
    thus we cannot stand still amid the sins of inhumanity.

We are marching for freedom:
    freedom from human exploitation
    and freedom from the cancerous sin of racism.
In the urban metropolises,
    in the rural farm areas
    we are marching.

We are marching for justice;
    for there is no justice for the poor,
    no justice for thy people.
We are praying to thee, O God,
    as we join hands and tread thy narrow path;
    for wherever thy people are seeking liberation,
    we are marching.

I Pray in Thanksgiving

Most gracious God, my liberator and savior,
   in all humility I come to thee in vocal prayer;
   I pray in thanksgiving.
I give thanks to thee, O God,
   for you have sustained my life on this earthly plane with
      thy love and grace.
I give thanks to thee, O God,
   for you have comforted my family and comrades
   amid the sufferings and sacrifices that we have
      experienced.
To thee, O Creator, I give gratitude
   for you have heard the cry of my people
   who are struggling for survival.

Thank you God,
   thank you for thy protection
   and for thy living spirit.
Thank you for opening my eyes that I may see;
   for opening my heart that I may love,
      thank you God.

In the Morning They Came for Angela

O God of love, hear my prayer;
  bear witness to my testimony;
  hear this psalm concerning my beloved sister.
The prophecy of thy prophet james baldwin has come to be
    realized:
  "If they come in the morning for Angela
  they will be for us in the evening."

The racist oppressors hunted and searched;
  distributed her name on the f b i ten-most-wanted list;
  early in the morning they came for angela davis.
And why, dear God, did they draw their guns . . .
  why did they shackle, chain, and imprison her . . .
  why did they come for angela?

Grant me thy understanding;
  render thy people oppressed a new awakening;
  help us all to learn from what happened to our sister.
We had faith in thee, O God;
  we knew that thou wouldst show us thy light of struggle;
  but many of thy people questioned our direct actions for
    justice.

Should we not have challenged this persecution . . .
    should we not have taken an organized stand for our
        sister. . .
    should we not have spoken out in her behalf?
Yes, we knew then and now that the struggle to free angela
    was a struggle symptomatic and symbolic of the plight
    of all the oppressed national minorities in america.

We can testify, O God;
    we can truly acknowledge that in the same repressive
        vengeance
    the oppressors came for us in the evening.
We were surrounded at the point of shotguns . . .
    shackled, chained, and imprisoned . . .
    victimized in the historic tradition of the united states.

Who will they be for next . . .
    how many more political prisoners will there be . . .
    when they come again will we be better prepared?
God, we still have faith in thee;
    we pledge to continue thy struggle
    against the sins of oppression.

Human Rights

Unto thee, O God of justice, I call out;
  hear my question;
  lend thine ear to the outcry of thy people oppressed.
Where is there justice?
  Where is there human freedom?
  Where are human rights?

Answer me, O God of justice, answer me;
  let me hear thy forceful voice;
  let me feel thy strong presence.
Through struggle I have come to know that human rights are
    God-given;
  human rights are indivisible and inalienable.

Yet, O God of justice, there are many
  who preach human rights,
  who verbalize mere rhetoric.
Gross hypocrisy is the norm in the united states of america
  from the pulpit of the white house
  to the altars of the pentagon.

Where are human rights?
  Where is there human freedom?
  Where is there justice?
Amid the ongoing violations of all
  fundamental human rights,
  where do the people of God stand?

Somehow, O God, by continuing to ask thee this nagging
   question over and over again,
   the answer may be revealed.
We who have faith in thy power and in thy mighty hand
   understand our collective responsibility.

We know, dear Lord, that thy gift of human rights
   is found and maintained
   by thy will.
Further, O God, we know that thou hast commanded us
   to struggle in the interest of the
   oppressed.

Where are human rights?
   In thee, O God, we struggle for the fulfillment
   of all thy gifts.

Where is there human freedom?
   In thee, O God, we struggle to free ourselves
   from all the sins of evil.

Where is there justice?
   In thee, O God of justice, we struggle;
   in thee, O God of righteousness.
Human rights are for all thy people who give of themselves
   in the love
   and concrete sacrifice of struggle.

Let There Be Peace on Earth

O God, block the path of the warmongers;
    stand in the way of armies of imperialism;
    prevent the destruction of humanity and nature.
O God, let there be peace on earth;
    let there be more love and less hate;
    let there be more reconciliation and less social conflict.

Help us, O God, to eliminate the threats of war;
    give us courage to do away with all weapons of death;
    assist us in rebuilding the peace movement
    throughout the world.
Let our hands do the work of peace;
    let our spirits be united in purpose;
    let our souls be spared from the hell of war.

Speak, O God, to all the world's inhabitants;
    command an eternal cease-fire;
    issue the ultimate call to halt the madness of oppression.
Penetrate the armor of all oppressors, O God;
    break through the fortifications of evil;
    make a way for nonviolence.

O God, let there be peace on earth;
    let there be a continuing manifestation of thy love;
    let there be an everlasting presence of thy grace.
Peace among all the peoples of the world
    is the work and yearning of the oppressed
    as we all struggle anew to be free.

Remember Henry Marrow

We remember henry marrow
  for he was a good brother;
  he was a young black man.
O God, we remember how our brother was taken
  away from the community
  and sent to wrongly fight in Vietnam.

We remember henry marrow
  from oxford, north carolina,
  from africa but born in america.
O God, we remember that he went away
  to church every sunday;
  to mary potter school every day.

Yet O God, the thing about henry that we all should
  never forget
  is his victimization by racism.
We remember henry marrow
  who saluted the american flag
  and proudly wore an army uniform.

Henry came back to oxford
  to work and to build a family,
  to live and to die.
O God, the memory of what happened
  to henry marrow is still fresh in our minds,
  souls, and hearts.

After surviving the unjust vietnam horror,
   henry could not survive
   the genocidal horror of america.
O God, did you hear him scream
   when the white men shot him in the back
   and beat him in the head?

O God of mercy, did you hear henry marrow
   scream out to beg
   the men named teel?
Henry begged them not to kill him;
   he pleaded for his life
   as they surrounded him.

O God of love, did you hear
   the white man say to his son,
   "shoot the nigger"?
We remember henry marrow
   for he was a good brother;
   he was a young black father.

Free Nelson Mandela

Way down in south africa's land
on a small prison island
there is an african leader held prisoner.
Free nelson mandela, O God of justice;
break the chains
of his unjust imprisonment.

For a quarter century on robbin's island,
nelson has been in the inhuman prison cells
of the oppressive south africa regime.
O God of justice, help us to tear down
the walls of the prison island,
to dismantle the structures of apartheid.

Free nelson mandela and all political prisoners;
let freedom ring in africa
and everywhere on earth.
Through struggle, O God, through struggle
with thy power and might
we shall free nelson mandela.

Who Dropped the Bombs on Hiroshima and Nagasaki?

Tell me clearly, O God;
  stir up my soul;
  disturb my complacency.
Answer me, dear God:
  who dropped the bombs
  on hiroshima and nagasaki?

What nation of the world
  would attempt to destroy another
  through nuclear radiation?
What nation of the world
  that claims to be under God
  would destroy God's creation?

What manner of greed,
  what manner of hate,
  what manner of inhumanity?
Who dropped the bombs, O God,
  can we stop them
  from dropping the bombs again?

From Soweto to El Salvador

From soweto to el salvador, O God,
  from johannesburg to harlem
  thy people are oppressed.
O God, from chile to namibia,
  from watts to the philippines
  thy people are suffering.

Let the organized masses of thy people
  who are oppressed
  rise up with thee, O God.
Let the victims of imperialism,
  the victims of colonialism
  and neocolonialism rise up unified.

Sometimes, O God, it is difficult
  to struggle without fighting back;
  it is hard to love the enemy.
Yet, O God, we have faith
  that thou wilt help us struggle
  from soweto to el salvador.

Chains and Leg Irons

O God, help me!
O God, help me!
The weight of these chains
and the pain of these leg irons
are unbearable.

O God, help me!
O God, help me!
The weight of these chains
and the pain of these leg irons
are unbearable.

O God, help me!
O God, help me!
The weight of these chains
and the pain of these leg irons
are unbearable.

Cynthia, Denise, Carol, and Addie

Dear God, it is september 15
I wonder, O God,
how many people still remember . . .
what day this is.

O God of justice, O God of peace
hear my prayer
hear my cry
hear my scream

It is this prison cell
it is my blackness
it is my faith
that causes me to remember . . .

Cynthia wesley, 14 years old
denise mcnair, 11 years old
carol robertson, 14 years old
and addie mae collins, 14 years old

O God, these thy children
black girls
went to sunday school
on september 15, 1963.

O God, our little sisters
went to the 16th street baptist church
down in birmingham, alabama
our little sisters . . .

Bless them, O God,
that kind of hate
that destroyed
our little sisters
is still around

O God, it is september 15
I wonder, O God,
how many people still remember
what day this is.

The National Alliance

Help the national alliance, O God,
help us free
all political prisoners.

Our alliance is against
racist and political repression
we are for freedom and justice.

Dear God, through mass struggle
we can win
peoples' victories.

Unity is the solution . . .
freedom is a constant struggle
basta la represión!

Inspiration to Keep On

I like the songs of aretha franklin
   like the poetry of saundra sharpe
   like the vibrations of james brown
   like the sounds of struggle
   like the winds of victory
   like the sermon on the mount
   like the gospel of Jesus Christ
   like all of God's people.

Thank you God, for helping me
   to like life . . .
   never seen freedom
   but I like it
   to like, to be positive
   gives
   inspiration to keep on.

Woe unto the Capitalists

Woe unto the capitalists
who monopolize workers
who in greed
choke the economy
who pay no taxes
choke the poor
who aid south africa
choke the third world
who build bombs to drop
choke humanity.

Woe unto the greedy capitalists
for the wrath of God
shall come upon them.

Sistuhs and Brotuhs

O God, Creator! O God, Redeemer!
lend thine ear
hear this psalm.

O God, help us to know
that we are all
sistuhs and brotuhs.

Amid the polarization of races,
sexes, and classes
we are still of one God.

O God, help us to know
that we are all
sistuhs and brotuhs.

Blessed Are the
Freedom Fighters, II

Blessed are the freedom fighters
who risk their lives
in the interest of human liberation.

Blessed are the freedom fighters
who give of themselves
to save others.

Blessed are the freedom fighters
who organize
who obey God's word.

Blessed are the freedom fighters
who pray
and keep the faith.

Blessed are the freedom fighters
who fight
and who win.

Steve Biko

O God, my brother steve biko . . .
   we went on a hunger strike together
   I in north carolina
   he in south africa

Dear God, let thy strong hand
   stop the continued
   murder of our people
   in north carolina
   and in south africa.

The struggle will intensify
   let us be prepared
   let us be ready
   let us thank God
   for the struggle

Remember steve biko.

Let My People Go

Mr. president, I have a message for you;
  it is a message sent directly to you
  and to all the ruling class;
  it is a message to all tyrants,
  to all imperialists, capitalists, and racists;
  it is a message to all oppressors,
  to all corporate exploiters.
Thus saith the God of all:
  "Let my people go!"

Mr. president, I know that you
  and all the ruling class
  do not want to hear the message;
  I know from experience that you
  do not hear very well the cries of the oppressed
  I pray that you will hear this warning
Thus saith the God of all:
  "Let my people go!"

Pharaoh! . . . from my prison cell
  I can hear the command of God
  I can see the vision of mass struggle
  I can sense the irreversible momentum
  I can feel the irrepressible activity
  of the oppressed people of God
  who shall surely rise up to freedom.
The mighty voice of the God of all saith:
  "Let my people go!"

Pharaoh! . . . in my prison cell
    faith in God still exists . . .
    faith in the freedom struggle
    faith in the justice seekers
    faith in the power of God
    soon and very soon
    the mighty crowd of God shall march.
Pharaoh! . . . . Pharaoh! . . . .
    "Let my people go!"

PART III

Liberation

Jesus the Liberator

To the poor
to the oppressed
to all those who are exploited . . .
Jesus Christ
is the liberator
for
the active struggle
confronting
the evils of america
and the world
the liberator
is
Jesus

Christs the Center

Christ
is the center
of my life
Christ
is the vertex
of my soul
Christ
is the spirit
that holds me together
in times
of trial and tribulation
Christ
is the center
of the freedom struggle
that is why
victory is certain
because
Christ is the center.

The Holy Spirit

The Holy Spirit
is upon the prison cell
the Holy Spirit
is upon me
the Holy Spirit
commands
freedom
justice
perseverance.

Where Do We Go from Here?

O God
O Christ Jesus
Where do we
go from here
but onward
bearing the cross
where do we
go from here
to die
or
to live?

Jesus Is the One

Jesus is the one
who can sustain every pain
Jesus is the one
who can turn wrong into right
Jesus is the one
who can hold you up
when you are about to fall
Jesus is the one
who can enable one
to struggle
to fight
to be free.

Shake the Iron Bars

O God
Shake this jail cell
rock this cement boat
O God of power
Shake the iron bars
away
from
the dungeons
of
hell on earth
shake the iron bars
away.

Pontius Pilate Is Still Governor

O God
it has been a long time
but pontius pilate
is still governor
every day
attempting to wash
the hands of the system
of racism and capitalism
clean
of all wrongdoing
but
we know their
hands are still dirty
it has been a long time
pilate is still governor.

Jesus Is the Light

Jesus is the light
of the struggle
of the oppressed
Jesus is the light
for all those
who seek justice
Jesus is the light
for all those
who love mercy
Jesus is the light
for all those
who will let
their own light shine.

Justice Delayed

Justice delayed
is no justice
at all
for God
is the great
judge
of all humanity
and God demands
that justice
roll down
swiftly
and equitably.

I Have a Vision

I have a vision
O God
I have a vision
of the eventual
triumph
of the poor and oppressed
over the oppressors
of the world . . .
love will conquer hate
humanity will survive
but we must
"wait upon the Lord"
which means
we must struggle on
until the second coming.

Stop the Draft

O God
stop the draft
for war . . .
teach us, O God
how to make peace
not war . . .
O God
stop the draft
put an end
to the war
machine.

The Keys to Freedom

The keys to freedom
are
know thy God . . .
know thyself
know thy freedom movement
know thy victory
the keys to freedom
come from God
the keys to freedom
are won through struggle.

Thank You God

Thank you God for allowing me to be alive
thank you God for giving me bread to eat
thank you God for the air that I breathe
thank you God for the water that I drink
thank you God for the sunshine
thank you God for the stars and the moonlight
thank you God for the trees
thank you God for the green grass and the brown soil
thank you God for all that you continue to do for me
thank you God that I'm able to survive the torment of this
    prison cell
thank you God for allowing me to see freedom again
one day soon.

Run the Robbers Out

Well Jesus
the robbers are back in the temple again
many of those who claim to be born again
are using a false faith
to materially profit in thy temple
come Jesus
come Jesus
come Jesus
run the robbers out.

Jesus Can Heal the Sick

Jesus can heal the sick
if the sick have faith
for faith is a determining factor
in every process of healing
Jesus can heal the sick
sometimes out of the love of God
when there is no faith
but hopefully after the sick are well
they will remember that Jesus can heal the sick.

Christopraxis Struggle/Liberation

Christopraxis struggle/liberation
involves
letting Christ be the center
not only of one's faith affirmation
but also one's activity in life
praxis is practicing
one's faith
to practice faith in Jesus Christ
surely will bring
struggle
and liberation.

Jesus Is Love

Jesus is love
because God is love
Jesus is love
because God so loved the world
that Jesus was sent in love
for love
Jesus is love
breaks open the eternal possibility
for love
to be for all
because Jesus is love.

Peace Be Still

Peace be still
O God of the universe
hear the rage of thy people crying out
for a moment
of peace . . .
peace of mind
no longer worrying about the problem
but at peace
with ourselves
in order to advance the struggle
progressively forward
don't worry . . .
struggle . . .
don't be so upset
you can't
struggle . . .
one day at a time, O God
now and forever
peace be still.

Holy Trinity

Holy, holy, holy . . .
O God of justice
O Son of humanity
O Spirit of love
come by here
come by here to assist thy people
in a battle for life
in a quest for freedom
Holy, holy, holy . . .
God come
Jesus Christ come
Holy Spirit come
together in unity
together in Holy Trinity
Holy, holy, holy . . .
Now
right now, O God
break the chains of oppression
now.

The Crucifixion

The crucifixion continues . . .
like they did it to Jesus, O God,
they continue to do it to thy people
using modern technology of death
but as they crucified
our Lord
they did not understand
the power of God
that overrides human finitude . . .
we rejoice
because on the third day
early in the morning
Jesus was raised up . . .
O God in Christ
let there be
continued resurrections
amid
the continued crucifixions . . .
thank you, dear God.

The Resurrection

The truth
shall always
rise again
the truth is Jesus resurrected
the truth is the people of God
continuing
the resurrection
up from the tombs of oppression
up from the urban cement caves
the resurrection
continuing
in our lives
in our souls
forever
because Jesus
is with us
in the eternal struggle of life:
the resurrection.

Push Forward for Justice

We must together with Jesus Christ
by our side
push forward for justice
in all the halls and courts
wherever our people are
victimized
and treated unjustly
we must together
push forward for justice
even when it may appear
too unpopular
we are called by God
we are called to push forward
for justice
loving-kindness
and for human fairness
we must together
push forward for justice.

Can't Turn Around Now

There ain't no way
we can stop now
we all have been through
too many trials and tribulations
to stop
we will not retreat
we will not give up hope
for God does act in human history
therefore we
can't turn around now
no, not now
no, not ever
the struggle of Jesus is lifelong
in fact
it is everlasting
therefore we
can't turn around now.

Jesus Is My Brother

I am an african
and
Jesus is my brother
I know Jesus to be my personal
liberator
the sustaining force
of my existence
as a minister
as a freedom worker
as a prisoner
yet still in the struggle
Jesus is my brother
as I walk down freedom's road
Jesus walks with me
as I sit in this prison cell
Jesus sits with me
because
Jesus is my brother.

The Fellowship

Blessed be the fellowship
where collective love exists
where a human sharing is manifest
blessed be the fellowship
of Jesus Christ
sisters and brothers of the Lord
making a way
out of no way
all to the glory of God . . .
blessed be the fellowship
where there is no jealousy
or envy
blessed be the fellowship
of Jesus Christ
for they will be able
to withstand
the oppression at hand
blessed be the fellowship.

The Faithful Community

The church
the faithful community
of believers in Jesus Christ
who come together
to worship God
to confess sin
to share in everything
who come together
to take a stand for justice
peace and liberation . . .
the faithful community
the church of Christ
continues
to the remnant
existing and struggling
to reconcile the world
unto God.

God Moves

God moves
in all of human history
God moves
on the side of the oppressed
God moves in Jesus Christ
to liberate
to justify
to sanctify
God moves through prison walls
to comfort
to sustain
to free
God moves on all levels
simultaneously
God moves.

Not Long

Not long
black people
not long
suffering will not last always.
how long?
not long because Jesus
is the liberator
how long?
forever . . .
what we need to do
is to practice our faith
in our lives
as well as the words
we speak . . .
it will be
not long
before the revolution comes
not long
are you ready
not long . . .

Keep On Keeping the Faith

Brothers and sisters
we just got to
keep on keeping the faith
the spirit of the Lord is with us
in struggle
for liberation . . .
O God, we are steadfast
in our faith in Jesus
in our struggle
in the interest
of all thy people oppressed
and
if we have learned anything
over the many years
we have learned
that
we just got to
keep on keeping the faith.

Righteousness

For righteousness' sake . . .
thy people, O God
are being persecuted . . .
righteousness is the parameter
it is the norm
it is the goal
objectified in Jesus Christ . . .
righteousness is poor people
not being poor . . .
righteousness is hungry people
not being hungry no more . . .
righteousness is a process . . .
the process of liberation.

Love

Love is simple . . .
if it is complex
then it is not love . . .
love is giving . . .
if it is receiving
then it is not love . . .
love is liberating . . .
if it is oppressing
then it is not love . . .
love is good . . .
if it is bad
then it is not love . . .
love is a gift from God
Jesus Christ loves
we sometimes are not open
to love
one another
but God loves us anyway
God's love is prevenient
love.

Which Way to Heaven?

Which way to heaven?
there is only one way . . .
only
through
Jesus Christ
can one find heaven . . .
the path is narrow
yet the passage
is free
only
through
Jesus Christ.

Today

Today is the right time
to call on God
to involve oneself in the liberation
of all God's people
from oppression . . .
today is God's day
the peoples' day
who take a stand on justice
and freedom
today is better
than tomorrow if you want
to stand up
for what is right in the world
and that is Jesus Christ
that is with the oppressed
today is the day.

Forever

Forever, O God
I pledge my life to thee
in service
in ministry
in struggle
forever is a long time
but it is necessary
to win the ultimate victory
forever, O God
I pledge my life to thee
in gratitude
in humility
in faith
forever, O God,
I will love thee.

God Shall Be Praised

God
shall be praised
for God
has brought us this far
along the journey of life
up from slavery
down with modernity
we say aloud
that God will always
have our praises
for
God
shall be praised
shall be lifted up
for
God is real . . .
real good for all who believe
God shall be praised
all the days of my life
all the days of the struggle
all the moments to come
God shall be praised!

EPILOGUE

I affirm that ultimate justice, liberation, and freedom
come only through the liberating activity of God in Jesus
Christ. There is evil in the world: racism, economic exploitation, oppression, and genocide. The problem of theodicy
is real. Yet I believe from my own experiences that the
goodness and power of God can transform and override human evil. The preceding psalms express my concrete faith
in God and in the potential power of God's people organized
and mobilized in the struggle for freedom. The psalms are
statements of faith, analysis, and commitment. The prophetic critical voice of the Christian church should never
become silent, especially in the midst of human suffering
and oppression. Through faith and praxis in Jesus Christ as
Liberator, we shall overcome.

On December 4, 1980, the Fourth Circuit United States
Court of Appeals in Richmond, Virginia overturned the unjust conviction of the Wilmington Ten. The Wilmington Ten
were freed and vindicated as a result of struggle and as a
result of keeping an active praxis-faith in God.

May these psalms continue to speak to all humanity in the
interest of simple justice and the complete liberation of all
oppressed peoples.